BETTER THAN AVERAGE

DR. ADAM LINK

DR. ADAM LINK
More Light Press
From the Iron Range in MN

Printed Worldwide
First Printing 2025
First Edition 2025

10 9 8 7 6 5 4 3 2 1

ISBN: 978-1-959850-07-6

Interior Book Design by Walt's Book Design
www.waltsbookdesign.com

BETTER THAN AVERAGE

TABLE OF CONTENTS

CHAPTER 1

THE CULT OF AVERAGE

"What gets measured gets managed," the old saying goes. But what if what we're measuring is the wrong thing altogether?

In today's world of financial advice, success is most often defined by a single comparison: did your portfolio beat the benchmark? The S&P 500, a 60/40 stock-bond blend, or a similar yardstick becomes the anchor for every conversation. If the portfolio outperformed, the year was a success. If it lagged, something must be fixed. This comparison is so ingrained, so rarely questioned, that it has become a kind of gospel. But therein lies the danger—because benchmarks, while useful, are descriptive tools. They explain what happened to a broad category of assets. They don't prescribe what an individual investor should do, nor do they guarantee a successful outcome. And yet, financial planners have elevated these benchmarks from tools to commandments, reducing complex, personal goals to one simplistic question: did we beat the market?

This is the Cult of Average. And it's distorting everything.

To understand how we got here, we need to acknowledge the original purpose of benchmarks. They weren't born as dogma. They emerged with good intentions—as a way to help investors evaluate whether their managers were adding value. If a mutual fund charged hefty fees and couldn't even match a basic index, what was the point? This critique was not only valid, it was essential. It sparked a wave of accountability that exposed underperforming funds and lowered costs across the board. It also paved the way for indexing, democratizing access to the markets for everyday investors. But as often happens, a good idea was taken too far.

Somewhere along the way, the benchmark stopped being a measuring stick and became the plan itself. Advisors didn't just compare portfolios to the S&P—they began constructing portfolios that mimicked it. Deviations from the index were now seen as risky or irresponsible. The job shifted from crafting a strategy to managing tracking error. In this new paradigm, consistency—not excellence—became the goal.

The consequences of this shift are subtle but severe. When advisors aim to match a benchmark, they start redefining success in narrow, impersonal terms. Consider a client who wants to retire at sixty, avoid major losses along the way, and convert their savings into a reliable stream of retirement income. A benchmark-minded advisor might design a portfolio that returns exactly 7.4% annually—the historical average of a balanced portfolio. On paper, it checks every box. But what if that return came with a brutal 38% drawdown just two years before retirement? What if the portfolio never recovered in time? What if withdrawals had to begin at market lows, cementing permanent losses?

In that case, beating the benchmark wouldn't matter at all. The client's goals would still be shattered. That's the central flaw of the Cult of Average: it prizes relative performance over actual outcomes. It makes winning on paper more important than delivering results in the real world.

So how did we get here? The answer lies in a mix of incentives and institutional training. Most advisors are educated within frameworks like the CFP curriculum, which emphasizes historical averages and long-term market returns. Volatility, they're taught, is normal. Staying the course is always the right move. Compliance departments reinforce this thinking. Benchmark tracking is easy to defend in audits and lawsuits. If everyone else is doing it, it's hard to get in trouble for doing the same. Custodians and platforms offer plug-and-play models that mirror broad indexes. They're cheap, simple, and scalable. Even the media joins in. Every headline about "the market" uses the S&P 500 as a proxy. A portfolio that diverges too far from the benchmark is often framed as rogue, risky, or out of touch.

And so, without meaning to, the industry trains advisors to aim low. To build portfolios that are good enough rather than actually good. To avoid deviation rather than seek excellence. To prioritize simplicity over strategy.

This wouldn't be so dangerous if average outcomes were sufficient. But they're not. Not for clients with real goals and real risks. Consider what happens when an investor experiences two recessions in the five years leading up to retirement. Or when inflation eats away at fixed-income yields. Or when market dynamics change in a way that breaks the assumptions of historical averages. Matching the benchmark in those scenarios isn't a win. It's a failure dressed in acceptable numbers.

It's worth pausing to ask: would we accept this logic in other areas of life? Would you hire a doctor who treats every patient with the same average dosage? Would you respect a personal trainer who promises you'll be exactly as healthy as the average American? Of course not. In most professions, "average" is not the goal. It's the floor. It's what you settle for when you can't do better. But in investing, we've turned it into a virtue.

There are also hidden costs to this obsession with tracking benchmarks. It encourages underreaction in volatile environments. When inflation surged in 2021 and 2022, many portfolios stayed locked into long-duration bonds because that's what the model called for. It discourages adaptation. Advisors who explore macro-driven or tactical strategies often face scrutiny—not because those strategies are flawed, but because they don't hug the benchmark tightly enough. It stifles innovation. New approaches, particularly those that prioritize risk management or drawdown control, are penalized for being different.

And worst of all, it ignores the client. A retiree who loses $200,000 in a "good" year—because the loss was smaller than the benchmark—doesn't feel successful. They feel afraid. They feel vulnerable. They feel like the plan failed. Because it did.

So what should we measure instead?

The answer isn't another index. It's a shift in mindset. We should measure maximum drawdown—because how deep the portfolio falls matters more than how fast it climbs. We should track recovery time—because the difference between a two-year recovery and a seven-year one can determine whether retirement starts on time. We should evaluate tax efficiency, cash flow reliability, and inflation sensitivity. Most importantly, we should measure the client's progress toward their own goals, not just their portfolio's proximity to an index.

This kind of planning is harder. It doesn't fit neatly into a dashboard. It resists standardization. But it's the only way to deliver real value. And it's the only way to escape the gravitational pull of average.

Benchmarks still have a role to play. They can be useful diagnostics. But they should never be the destination. The real question isn't "Did we beat the market?" It's "Did we build a portfolio that serves this client's life?" That's a higher bar. It requires more work, more nuance, more courage. But that's what the job demands.

The Cult of Average is seductive. It offers safety, simplicity, and a shared language. But great advice isn't about being safe. It's about being effective. It's about designing strategies that are resilient, not just compliant. Personalized, not just scalable.

It's time to stop worshipping benchmarks—and start building better outcomes.

CHAPTER 2

THE TRUTH ABOUT "I DON'T KNOW"

There's a phrase you hear constantly in financial circles, repeated like gospel: "We don't know where the market is going." It's delivered with an air of humility, as if restraint were wisdom and uncertainty a virtue. At first glance, it seems grounded—like the mature voice in the room refusing to make wild predictions. But more often than not, it's a shield. A way to shut down the conversation before it gets uncomfortable. A way to avoid responsibility for hard calls. A way to deflect, not inform.

To be clear, admitting uncertainty isn't wrong. In fact, it's essential. But what comes after "I don't know" is what separates the amateurs from the professionals. The mistake is in stopping there. Because in finance—as in medicine, aviation, or engineering—we often can't predict the future, but we can prepare for it. A good doctor won't pretend to know precisely which illness a patient will develop in the next year, but they can identify risk factors. They can recommend lifestyle changes based on labs, family history, and early indicators. They don't know everything, but they know enough to act. That's not arrogance. That's professionalism.

Finance should work the same way. Markets are not chaotic dice rolls. They are complex, adaptive systems. They have memory. They trend. They revert. They warn. You don't need to be clairvoyant to notice the signals. You just need to pay attention. Valuations stretch. Momentum builds or fades. Credit spreads widen. Volatility clusters. Central banks shift posture. These are not crystal balls. They are dashboards.

Yet, the overwhelming norm in retail advisory is to ignore them. Advisors are taught—sometimes implicitly, sometimes explicitly—that recognizing these signals is outside their domain. That it's speculative. Dangerous. Irresponsible. The safe route is to be agnostic. To never make a call. To ride the wave no matter how stormy, because at least then you're not swimming alone. But there's an irony here that's hard to ignore: by pretending to avoid risk, we often create more of it.

Blind agnosticism is not safety. It's passivity.

There's a vital difference between making predictions and making preparations. Between claiming certainty and acting on probability. The best advisors don't need to guess next year's S&P return. They just need to know that certain patterns precede certain conditions. For instance, they know that when the VIX—a measure of volatility—spikes above 30, forward returns tend to be choppy. They know that high equity valuations compress future return potential. They know that when earnings revisions turn negative across sectors, pressure builds beneath the surface. They know that an inverted yield curve, coupled with deteriorating PMIs, is not just a trivia item—it's a signal. These insights don't guarantee outcomes. But they tilt the odds.

Investing, at its core, is not about being right all the time. It's about positioning intelligently when the environment changes. Think of it like driving on a mountain road. A weather alert pops up: black ice ahead. You don't know exactly where it is. But you slow down. You drive differently. You adjust. You don't ignore the alert because you can't locate the ice on a map. You act on the probability.

That's what good investing feels like. It's not clairvoyance. It's caution paired with clarity.

And yet, the modern advisor often refuses to take the wheel. Not because they can't—but because they've been taught not to. The CFP curriculum doesn't train planners in macroeconomic analysis. Most planning software assumes fixed return rates, calculated from historical averages. Risk is defined by standard deviation—an abstract measure—rather than by anything the client actually experiences. So when the market tilts or trembles, the default response is to rebalance and repeat the mantras: "Time in the market, not timing the market." "Stay the course." "Volatility is normal."

But volatility is only normal if your client's life is, too. If they don't need to retire next year. If they don't panic and sell. If they don't need liquidity when the market is down. If they can afford to wait. Otherwise, volatility is risk. Real risk. Not just variance on a chart, but emotional, behavioral, and practical exposure.

Imagine a different kind of advisor. One who says, "I don't know where the market will be next quarter—but I know valuations are in the 95th percentile, and we should think about reducing exposure." Or, "I can't tell you when the next recession starts, but the leading indicators are flashing yellow. Let's get more defensive." Or even, "We're not trying to beat the market. We're trying to sidestep its worst stretches."

That kind of advisor isn't promising magic. They're promising vigilance.

The irony is, data-driven investing doesn't mean high-frequency trading or watching tickers all day. It just means staying awake. Too many portfolios are built like autopilot systems—perfectly engineered for clear skies, but helpless in turbulence. We would never accept this in other professions. Pilots adjust for crosswinds. Surgeons adapt to bleeding. CEOs pivot when supply chains break. But advisors? Many sit frozen, armed only with a smile and a spreadsheet, waiting for the storm to pass.

And often it does. But not always. Sometimes it crashes a retirement plan. Sometimes it knocks a nervous client out of the market for a decade. Sometimes it costs years of compounding. That's not theoretical. It's happened, over and over, from 2000 to 2002, from 2008 to 2009, from March 2020. And it will happen again.

The idea that "I don't know" absolves us from responsibility is seductive. It feels humble. It feels compliant. But used without discipline, it becomes a license for inertia. For shrugging instead of solving. For drifting instead of designing.

That's why great planning isn't about avoiding decisions. It's about pre-committing to smart ones. Structuring the playbook before the whistle blows. That's what active management, properly understood, really is. It's not a bet. It's a framework. A system of tilts, constraints, and rules that respond to conditions—not emotions.

We do this in every other facet of life. We adjust our calories when our metabolism changes. We reevaluate business strategy when margins fall. We check the weather before planning a road trip. None of that is guesswork. It's adaptation. And it works.

So why, in the one domain where our entire financial future lives, have we trained professionals to be passive?

Why, in the face of so many observable signals, have we built an industry that prides itself on inaction?

Because we've confused risk with responsibility. Because it's easier to lose in a crowd than to win alone. Because shrugging is scalable—and scalable is profitable.

But when it's your retirement on the line, your child's college fund, your financial independence—shrugging isn't a strategy.

Thinking is.

And thinking starts by replacing dogma with discipline, mantras with models, and fear of error with preparation for uncertainty. We don't need to know everything. But we need to act on what we do know. That's not market timing. That's just good planning.

Because not every storm can be predicted. But we can still build better boats.

Chapter 3

Data Exists—We Just Ignore It

Most investors—and, frankly, most advisors—walk through the markets like a tourist in a new city navigating with their eyes closed, guided only by a ten-year-old weather report. We claim to be rational. We claim to be planners. But our portfolios too often reveal something else: a deep, institutionalized commitment to inertia disguised as discipline.

We've built a profession that prizes consistency over context. When markets shift, we rebalance. When volatility spikes, we rebalance. When credit markets freeze or inflation accelerates or earnings estimates crater—we rebalance. Like a priest performing a ritual, we believe in the act itself more than the world around us. It's called staying the course. It's called avoiding market timing. But in practice, it's called doing nothing.

And it's all built on a myth: that the market is fundamentally unpredictable, and therefore any attempt to respond to changing conditions is not just fruitless, but foolish. This myth has become the silent scaffolding of most modern investment advice, passed from whitepapers to advisors to clients like a sacred truth.

This chapter is here to burn that scaffolding down.

Because here's the thing: data exists. And we ignore it at our peril.

Momentum exists. Volatility regimes exist. Macro indicators send signals. Drawdown probabilities can be modeled. Recessions don't arrive without warning. We may not be able to call the exact day or week of a correction, but pretending we can't see stress building is intellectually dishonest.

The foundation of the passive-only mindset—the idea that no one can predict the market—isn't entirely wrong. It's just overextended. Sure, we can't know the precise 12-month return of the S&P 500. But great investing doesn't require that level of clairvoyance. It requires adaptation, not prediction. The goal isn't to divine the future; it's to recognize the present with enough clarity to avoid avoidable risk and position wisely for what's likely.

Momentum, for instance, is not a fringe idea anymore. In 1993, Narasimhan Jegadeesh and Sheridan Titman published a seminal paper showing that stocks with strong recent performance tend to continue outperforming in the short term. This finding directly contradicted the Efficient Market Hypothesis, which holds that prices reflect all available information. But the momentum anomaly persisted. Follow-up studies by researchers like Moskowitz, Ooi, and Pedersen in 2012 expanded the evidence, showing momentum works across asset classes—equities, commodities, currencies, and bonds—even across different geographies. It wasn't just a U.S. equities phenomenon. It was universal.

You'd think this would be front and center in most advisor playbooks. Yet it's nearly invisible. Why? Because momentum doesn't sit still. It trades. It creates turnover. It violates style boxes and benchmark tracking. Advisors trained to fear deviation from the index rarely embrace a strategy that, by design, deviates often.

And momentum is just the beginning. Volatility clustering—the observation that markets tend to experience waves of calm followed by waves of turbulence—is another critical feature of financial markets. This was first introduced in Mandelbrot's work on fractals in the 1960s and later formalized through GARCH models by Bollerslev in 1986. More recently, researchers like Moreira and Muir demonstrated that portfolios which scale exposure based on volatility—taking risk down when volatility rises and increasing it in calmer markets—outperform static portfolios. Their 2017 study was a direct challenge to the "buy and hold forever" doctrine. The implication? Adjusting exposure based on regime shifts doesn't just reduce drawdowns. It enhances long-term returns.

Yet, again, most financial advisors are taught to ignore volatility completely. It's not in the basic risk profile questionnaire. It's not tracked in most planning software. It's seen as noise—something to endure rather than respond to. But investors don't experience risk as standard deviation. They experience it as drawdown. As panic. As regret.

And that's the other blind spot: drawdown modeling. Ask a room full of advisors to quote the average return of a portfolio, and many will have a precise number. Ask them for the probability of a 25% loss in the next twelve months, and you'll get blank stares. Standard deviation is neat. It fits into the Monte Carlo tools. But clients don't panic over deviation. They panic over losses. Andrew Lo's Adaptive Markets Hypothesis laid this bare—markets change behavior under stress. They evolve. The conditions under which risk is realized are not static. Treating them as such is academic malpractice.

Speaking of malpractice, imagine this: you're driving a car on a winding road. The windshield is painted black. You can't see out. But you're told not to worry—the average speed on this road is 45 miles per hour. Just keep your foot on the gas. That's what passive investing asks of clients. To drive blind, because historically, the average result has worked out.

But the dashboard is working just fine.

Yield curve inversions have preceded every U.S. recession of the last 50 years. Purchasing Manager Index (PMI) readings below 50 have historically signaled contraction in manufacturing activity. Credit spreads, especially the gap between high-yield bonds and Treasuries, widen before market stress. And composite indices like the Conference Board's Leading Economic Indicators flag softening conditions before the headlines catch up. These aren't obscure signals. They're published monthly. They're public. They're measurable.

And yet, most advisors do nothing with them.

This isn't about predicting the next 100-point move in the S&P. It's about preparing. In March 2020, as COVID fears exploded, the VIX spiked past 80. Most trend-following models turned risk-off. Volatility-sensitive portfolios de-risked. When the market bottomed and began its sharp rebound, these models didn't catch the bottom—but they avoided the worst of the crash and re-engaged soon after. Passive portfolios, in contrast, endured the full ride down and only recovered because the fiscal and monetary firehose saved the day.

That's the point: you don't need a perfect signal. You just need brakes that work.

Across the industry, there are practitioners quietly doing this well. Cambria's GMOM fund adjusts exposure based on global trend and momentum indicators. AQR's Style Premia strategies blend momentum, value, carry, and defensive signals systematically. ReSolve Asset Management uses machine learning and macro data to guide globally adaptive portfolios. These aren't get-rich-quick schemes. They're examples of planning done with eyes open.

So why aren't these approaches more widespread?

Because the incentives aren't aligned. Advisors aren't paid to innovate. They're paid to grow assets and avoid lawsuits. Passive portfolios are easy to scale, easy to defend, and easy to explain. They're the Costco of investing—good enough for most, but not tailored to anyone. And for many firms managing hundreds or thousands of clients, that's good enough.

But it shouldn't be. Not when better is available. Not when the data exists.

Ignoring momentum leaves alpha on the table. Ignoring volatility exposes clients to avoidable stress. Ignoring drawdown modeling sets retirees up for ruin. Ignoring macro signals means missing what's right in front of you.

This is not just a missed opportunity. It's a breach of professional duty.

Advisors don't need to become quants. But they do need to become awake. Read the macro dashboard. Track regime shifts. Measure drawdown risk. And most of all, build portfolios that respond to the environment—not just history.

Because the data is already there. The question is whether we'll finally open our eyes and use it.

CHAPTER 4

THE REAL RISK IS DRAWDOWN, NOT DEVIATION

Wall Street has a favorite obsession: volatility. Mention risk in any professional investment setting and you'll be met with a cascade of standard deviation metrics, quoted down to the second decimal place, as though that number captures the full essence of investor experience. It doesn't. In fact, it misses the mark entirely.

Because no client has ever called an advisor in a cold sweat and said, "My portfolio's deviation from the mean is unacceptably high." What they say—what they feel—is something very different: "I'm down 25%. Can I still retire?" That's not a volatility problem. That's a drawdown problem. And drawdown—not standard deviation—is the risk that really matters.

The financial industry has long preferred tidy mathematical constructs. Standard deviation is symmetric, elegant, and fits nicely into equations. It treats upside and downside with equal weight. A portfolio that gains 30% one year and loses 10% the next is treated the same—volatility-wise—as one that gains 10% and loses 10%. But the emotional experience of the investor is not the same. One feels like a rollercoaster that ends safely. The other feels like betrayal.

There is a deeper issue at play here. Losses compound against investors in nonlinear ways. A 50% loss isn't merely inconvenient—it's devastating. It requires a 100% gain just to break even. A 30%

loss needs a nearly 43% return to recover. Time and math don't cooperate easily in recovery mode. This asymmetry is why drawdowns deserve more attention than volatility measures ever receive.

Behaviorally, the consequences of drawdowns are enormous. Dalbar's 2023 Quantitative Analysis of Investor Behavior again confirmed what decades of studies have shown: there's a stubborn, persistent gap—often over 2% per year—between the returns of the market and the returns realized by investors. This isn't because of fees or bad funds. It's because people bail out at the wrong time. During drawdowns, fear takes the wheel. Investors sell at the bottom, sit on the sidelines, reenter too late, or chase what just went up. Drawdowns create a kind of behavioral gravity, pulling investors away from discipline. And over time, that behavioral drag silently erodes wealth.

If we define risk as the likelihood that a client will abandon their plan, then drawdowns are the number one risk—not volatility, not tracking error, not duration mismatches. The real enemy is the emotional response to large, sustained losses. Standard deviation does not measure this.

In academic circles, better tools exist. Conditional Value at Risk, or CVaR, offers a far more intuitive way to think about risk. Instead of treating the entire distribution of returns equally, CVaR focuses on the worst outcomes—the tail events. What's the average loss in the bottom 5% of market scenarios? That's CVaR. Rockafellar and Uryasev formalized it in 2000 as a tool for portfolio optimization, and by 2002, researchers like Krokhmal and Palmquist were demonstrating that minimizing CVaR leads to more downside-protected portfolios than traditional mean-variance optimization. Similarly, the Sortino ratio improves upon Sharpe by penalizing only downside volatility—something that actually aligns with how investors think.

Yet despite these advances, the financial planning software used in thousands of offices still proudly prints out reports filled with standard deviation and Sharpe ratios, leaving the metrics that actually matter to clients entirely off the page.

To understand the stakes, consider some real-world examples. During the Dot-Com Bust from 2000 to 2002, the NASDAQ fell a staggering 78% peak to trough. Tech-heavy investors were crushed. Even the broader S&P 500 fell nearly 50%. Standard deviation didn't help anyone avoid the loss, but plenty of indicators—valuation signals, deteriorating credit conditions, trend breakdowns—were available in real-time. Those who used them to de-risk preserved capital and optionality. Those who didn't were left with paper losses that turned into permanent ones.

Then came the Global Financial Crisis. From October 2007 to March 2009, global markets lost over half their value. A standard 60/40 portfolio still dropped 30%. Retirees felt the pain acutely. Imagine someone with $1.5 million in savings, drawing $75,000 annually. A 40% portfolio drop turns that plan from sustainable to unsalvageable almost overnight. The math stops working—not because of average returns, but because of sequence risk. As Pfau (2010) showed, it's not just the return that matters—it's when it happens. A bad year at the wrong time breaks the plan, even if the averages look fine on paper.

Even in the short-lived COVID crash of March 2020, markets fell 34% in just 23 trading days. The VIX spiked above 82. It was one of the fastest and most violent drawdowns in history. While the market rebounded quickly, many investors didn't. Retirees panicked. Withdrawals were paused. Positions were sold. Some never got back in. In contrast, funds with trend overlays or volatility targeting mechanisms adjusted quickly and recovered faster. As Corey Hoffstein documented, these adaptive portfolios didn't catch the bottom—but they sidestepped the worst of the fall.

These aren't theoretical risks. These are historical realities. They happened to real people, with real goals, at the worst possible times.

Drawdowns are especially dangerous for retirees. Because when you're withdrawing from a portfolio, a big drop early on doesn't just sting—it can compound into failure. This is sequence-of-returns risk. If the first few years of retirement feature steep losses, even strong long-term average returns won't save the plan. Wade Pfau and David Blanchett have both shown how early drawdowns dramatically increase the probability of portfolio ruin. The question facing retirees is not "Will the market return 8% on average?" It's "What happens if I'm down 30% right when I start taking money out?" That's the question that must be answered by advisors. And it can't be answered with standard deviation.

So how do we build portfolios that respect drawdown risk?

First, we must abandon the overreliance on Modern Portfolio Theory. MPT assumes normal distributions, mean-variance optimization, and static correlations. It assumes that risk is symmetrical and that returns cluster neatly around a bell curve. But the real world is messier. Drawdowns don't care about elegance.

Better approaches do exist. Maximum drawdown constraints can be embedded into optimization engines. Tools like Black-Litterman or robust optimizers allow for scenario modeling and explicit downside limits. Simple trend filters—like reducing equity exposure when an index falls below its 200-day moving average—can significantly reduce tail risk. Meb Faber's 2007 study showed that 10-month moving average filters lowered drawdowns without sacrificing long-term returns. More sophisticated trend models from Hurst, Ooi, and Pedersen further validated this in global portfolios during bear markets like 2008.

Volatility targeting is another powerful tool. By scaling exposure up or down based on market volatility, portfolios can smooth returns and reduce drawdowns. Moreira and Muir (2017) showed that these portfolios not only delivered higher Sharpe ratios but experienced fewer gut-wrenching drops.

And finally, tail risk hedging—using long volatility assets like options, managed futures, or dynamic put strategies—can create convexity in crises. As Ilmanen (2011) and Harvey & Siddique (2000) argued, these tools don't just defend against disaster—they can enhance performance when used thoughtfully.

Ultimately, the question isn't about performance at the top of the cycle. It's about durability through the bottom. Because that's what clients actually want. They don't sit in your office and ask for the highest Sharpe ratio or lowest tracking error. They ask: "Can I retire and stay retired?" "Can I handle another 2008?" "Will I be okay if we hit another crash?" These are drawdown questions. And they demand drawdown answers.

Advisors love to model for the average year. The average return. The average inflation rate. The average glidepath. But real life doesn't happen in averages. It happens in moments. And the wrong moment—a job loss, a recession, a health crisis—can undo years of planning.

We must stop designing portfolios that survive the typical year and start designing for the critical years—the ones that make or break a retirement plan.

Drawdowns are the silent killer. They don't show up in averages. They don't scream from pie charts. They don't raise alarms until it's too late. But they are always lurking. Always dangerous.

It's time financial advice matured. Volatility is a math problem. Drawdown is a life problem. Let's start designing for the right one.

CHAPTER 5

PASSIVE ISN'T SAFE—IT'S UNRESPONSIVE

Imagine standing on the coast, staring at the Atlantic Ocean, and someone hands you a boat and a map. They smile confidently and say, "Just let the current take you. It always works out eventually." Would you step in and shove off, trusting the tide with your life?

Most people wouldn't. They'd pause. They'd ask about storms, about icebergs, about fuel and weather and pirates. Yet this is exactly the kind of advice that has underpinned an entire era of financial strategy. The idea that markets "always go up" has become the modern tide chart, the reassuring myth that buoys passive investing. And it's time to snap out of it.

For more than a decade, passive investing felt like invincibility wrapped in simplicity. From 2010 through 2021, the S&P 500 posted strong double-digit returns. Every hiccup in the market proved temporary. Every scare rebounded. Every dip was a buying opportunity. The mantra of "stay the course" wasn't just soothing—it was rewarded. But that experience wasn't the result of some timeless truth. It was a product of a very specific environment: near-zero interest rates, unprecedented stimulus, disinflation driven by globalization, and the dominance of mega-cap tech companies. In that calm, passive investing looked brilliant.

That regime is over. Interest rates have snapped back. Inflation has proven sticky. Geopolitical tensions are rising, not retreating. And yet, millions of investors are still floating in the same passive boat—rudderless, unaware, and ill-prepared for the new currents.

The rise of passive investing was sold as empowerment. You no longer needed to rely on fund managers or pay high fees. Just buy the index. Stay invested. Let the market do the work. It sounded liberating. But in practice, passive investing trained people to disengage. It taught them to ignore the world around them, to dismiss macro indicators, to silence their own instincts. It didn't empower resilience. It fostered resignation.

And no other serious discipline behaves this way. Pilots don't fly through turbulence without intervention. Doctors don't treat heart attacks with routine checkups. Captains don't hold a steady course while storms rip through their ships. But in investing, we're told to do just that. Keep calm. Don't react. Trust the averages. This isn't discipline—it's stubbornness dressed up as rationality.

The most common defense of passive investing is its low cost. And yes, a 0.05% index fund usually beats a high-cost active fund when all else is equal. But cost isn't the only risk that matters. The deeper risk in passive portfolios isn't found in the expense ratio—it's in their unresponsiveness. These portfolios never raise cash. They never tilt away from danger. They never prepare for drawdown. They simply ride the market, regardless of the terrain ahead. That may be fine when the wind is at your back. But if the market turns, you're going with it.

Let's imagine a real investor. She's 62. Planning to retire in a year. She's saved $1.2 million in a 60/40 passive portfolio. Now suppose we experience a 35% drawdown—just like we did in 2008. Her portfolio loses $420,000. Her entire plan is jeopardized. Maybe her Social Security bridge strategy collapses. Maybe her projected retirement income falls below her baseline expenses. Maybe her spouse panics. Maybe she does too.

It's easy to say, "Well, the market came back." And yes, over time, it did. But if her life didn't come back with it—if the portfolio no longer fits the plan—what good is that historical fact? Passive investing only works if your timeline aligns with the market cycle. That's a massive, dangerous assumption. For many people, the market didn't recover in time. Their lives had already moved on.

Contrast that with the strategies employed by institutions and sophisticated asset managers. There is robust, well-documented evidence that responsiveness works. Trend-following strategies, as Hurst, Ooi, and Pedersen (2014) demonstrated, significantly outperformed during market crises. Volatility targeting, as shown in Moreira and Muir's 2017 study, both reduced drawdowns and improved compounded returns. Managed futures—often criticized for being complex—delivered strong positive returns in 2008, 2011, and 2022 when traditional stocks faltered, as noted by Greyserman and Kaminski (2014). Risk parity strategies, particularly those with macro overlays, outperformed traditional models during turbulent years, as published by Bridgewater and AQR. These are not fringe theories. These are institutional practices—used by pensions, endowments, sovereign wealth funds.

So why aren't retail investors using these techniques? Because they're hard to explain. They require nuance, discipline, and education. And they're harder to sell than "just buy and hold." But difficulty doesn't negate truth. We've simply lowered the bar.

Passive investing did democratize access. That's worth celebrating. It made broad diversification available at a fraction of the cost. But it also reshaped expectations. Instead of excellence, investors were taught to seek efficiency. Instead of planning around your life, portfolios were built around the market's long-term averages. Instead of hiring advisors to think, many firms outsourced investment management entirely to third-party models. If something underperforms? "Stay the course." If a client is nervous? "Don't worry, the market always goes up." That's not planning. That's shirking.

And if it's your money—your retirement, your family, your legacy—should you really accept that?

The point of working with a financial advisor is not to delegate conviction. It's to acquire better-informed conviction. A great advisor is not passive. A great advisor has a framework. A perspective. A way of processing risk that adapts when the landscape shifts. They don't blindly follow the market. They navigate it—with care, with intent, and with your life in mind. Yes, they charge more than 25 basis points. Because real work is being done. Portfolios are rebalanced dynamically. Asset allocations shift based on credit spreads, economic signals, or earnings revisions. Risk is managed actively, not endured passively. This isn't about timing tops and bottoms. It's about refusing to sit still when the storm hits.

Think back to the Global Financial Crisis. Investors who sold at the bottom in 2008 and missed the twelve months of rebound that followed never recovered, relative to dynamic portfolios that de-risked early and re-entered confidently. Imagine a client who had $1 million in 2007 and saw it fall to $500,000. Even if they didn't panic and sell, they may have frozen—failing to invest new cash or adjust their income plan. Meanwhile, portfolios with even basic trend filters softened the fall and shortened the path to recovery. That difference—between a halved balance and a preserved one—could be worth hundreds of thousands of dollars.

True safety isn't pretending storms don't exist. It's having the ability to steer through them. It means designing portfolios that recognize volatility. It means integrating macro signals. It means having contingency plans for inflation shocks, Fed pivots, earnings collapses. Passive investing tells you to hold your breath until the weather clears. Responsive investing hands you an oxygen mask.

Let's be clear: index funds are remarkable tools. But they are not strategies. They are the "what," not the "how," "when," or "why." A real plan may include index funds. But it will wrap them in systems that assess risk, adapt to change, and preserve what matters most—your capital, your income, your peace of mind.

You wouldn't drive a car without brakes or steering just because it costs less. Don't do that with your money.

The financial industry may be content handing out floaties and telling everyone to trust the tide. But you deserve better than that. You deserve a partner who tracks the weather, adjusts the sails, and keeps you on course—no matter what the market throws your way.

Because if your entire plan depends on the market always cooperating, you don't have a plan.

You have a hope.

And your life is too important to leave to hope.

CHAPTER 6

THE MATH OF MARGINAL GAINS

We often imagine successful investing as a product of rare genius or bold predictions. But what if the secret isn't clairvoyance or courage? What if it's something far less flashy—something small, quiet, and compounding? In truth, we don't need a crystal ball to win. We just need a margin. A modest, consistent edge. A 1–2% annual advantage, compounded over decades, doesn't look impressive in isolation. But over time, it becomes the difference between financial independence and financial anxiety. It's not noise. It's the whole game. And the greatest source of that edge? It's not picking the right stock or calling the top. It's drawdown control.

Losses are asymmetrical. A 10% decline requires an 11% gain to recover. A 20% drop takes 25%. If your portfolio drops 40%, you need a whopping 66.7% just to break even. And if you're unlucky enough to lose 50%, you'll need to double your money—100% growth—just to claw your way back to zero. These aren't subjective risks. They're math problems. Compounding only works when you protect the base it builds upon. Every dollar lost is a future dollar that can't compound. That's why drawdown control isn't about fear or conservatism. It's about math. The investor who loses less in the bad years doesn't need to win as much in the good ones to outperform. And over time, that arithmetic is destiny.

Let's talk about fees—the elephant that always stomps through any discussion of active management. Suppose your advisor charges

2.6% annually. That's a far cry from the sleek 0.05% index fund you saw lauded in a Reddit thread. And yet, what if that fee doesn't just buy you management—it buys you better results? Suppose that same advisor runs a strategy using macroeconomic models, volatility targeting, drawdown filters, or tactical tilts. And suppose that strategy delivers a consistent 1% to 1.5% improvement in your annualized net returns.

Sound implausible? It's not. A wealth of academic research supports the claim that modest, methodical risk management—especially strategies focused on avoiding tail events—can improve long-term results without requiring heroic performance.

Barroso and Santa-Clara (2015) examined volatility-managed portfolios and found they significantly outperformed their static counterparts across various asset classes. Especially during periods of crisis, the strategies that adjusted exposure based on volatility avoided catastrophic losses—and, importantly, recovered faster. Similarly, Hurst, Ooi, and Pedersen (2017) studied time-series momentum and found that applying trend-based filters led to higher Sharpe ratios and lower drawdowns across 134 years of market data. Kritzman and colleagues (2012) took it further, showing that adjusting risk based on regime changes produced better cumulative results with less volatility over four decades.

These weren't attempts to time the market. They weren't based on predictions. They were risk-aware systems designed to avoid catastrophic losses. They worked not by outperforming every year, but by staying intact when it mattered most. So the real question isn't, "Why does this cost more?" It's "What are you getting in return?"

Consider a simple case study: two investors, each starting with $1 million. One chooses a passive portfolio that earns 8% annually and charges 0.1% in fees. The other chooses an active strategy with a gross return of 7.2% and a fee of 2.6%. At first glance, it looks like the passive investor wins, netting 7.9% versus the active investor's 4.6%.

But now let's add a twist. In year five, there's a 40% market crash.

The passive portfolio drops from $1 million to $600,000. The active strategy—thanks to superior drawdown control—only falls 20%, landing at $800,000. Over the next 15 years, the passive investor compounds at 7.9% and ends with $1.93 million. The active investor, starting from a higher base and compounding at a slower 4.6%, ends with $1.98 million.

Despite higher fees and lower annual returns, the risk-managed portfolio wins. Why? Because it lost less when it mattered most. Marginal gains, applied strategically, beat brute strength—especially when the market turns.

And that's just during the accumulation phase. In retirement, drawdowns become even more lethal.

If you're in your thirties, you've got time to recover from bear markets. But if you're in your sixties and drawing from your portfolio, losses are amplified. This is the well-documented phenomenon known as sequence of returns risk. It's not just theoretical—it's devastating in practice.

Research by Pfau and Kitces (2014) found that retirees who experienced poor returns in their first five years had a dramatically higher chance of depleting their portfolios, even if their average long-term returns were identical to someone who experienced early gains. Translation: the order of returns can matter more than the returns themselves.

In this context, even slightly better downside protection can make the difference between a secure retirement and running out of money. A risk-aware portfolio that avoids steep early losses—even if it lags in bull markets—can dramatically increase your chances of long-term success.

But let's not pretend that investing is purely a math game. It's also a behavior game—and behavior compounds, too.

Every year, DALBAR releases its Quantitative Analysis of Investor Behavior. And every year, it shows the same result: individual investors underperform their own investments. In 2022, the gap was 3–4% annually, mostly due to emotional decisions. People sell during drawdowns. They buy high after a rally. They abandon long-term plans for short-term feelings.

Now imagine holding a portfolio that doesn't drop 35%. That doesn't spike your cortisol every time the VIX climbs. That reallocates calmly in stress periods or raises cash when needed. That kind of portfolio doesn't just protect your capital—it protects your discipline. And the value of not panicking? It might be the most important marginal gain of all.

To visualize this, let's run a basic 30-year compounding exercise. Two investors each save $30,000 annually from age 35 to 65. One earns 7% annually and ends up with roughly $2.84 million. The other earns 8.5% annually and ends with $3.94 million—a 38% increase from just a 1.5% improvement.

Now think about what that extra $1.1 million means. It could fund retirement three years earlier. It could mean leaving a more generous legacy. It might allow for a six-figure donation to a cause you care about. That's what marginal gains can do: not change your plan, but change how your plan ends.

The challenge? You rarely notice marginal gains in the moment. They're subtle. Boring. Invisible on any given Tuesday. They show up as small tilts: a slight underweight to overvalued sectors, a bond allocation shift before spreads widen, a pause in equity exposure when leading indicators deteriorate. They aren't bets. They're measured responses. And over time, they add up.

Of course, some years risk-managed portfolios will lag. You'll see headlines about index funds returning 24%, and you'll look at your statement and see 16%. You'll wonder, "Why am I paying more for less?" But that's the wrong question.

Investing isn't about maximizing short-term returns. It's about staying alive when others don't—and continuing to compound through uncertainty. Markets change. Volatility returns. Inflation surges. Pandemics hit. Crashes come fast and uninvited. You don't need to predict them. You need to survive them.

And that's the truth most investors miss: you don't need a miracle to transform your financial future. You don't need to beat the market by 10%. You don't need to find the next Tesla. You need a process that delivers 1% more discipline, 2% better defense, 1.5%

lower emotional drag—a framework that's designed to bend with the storm, not break under it. And ideally, an advisor who knows how to build that framework with intention.

Because great investing isn't heroic. It's incremental. It's measured. It's durable. And over time, it becomes extraordinary.

CHAPTER 7

HOW WE GOT HERE: THE ACADEMIC BAGGAGE

If you've ever worked with a traditional financial advisor or completed a financial planning course, odds are you've been steeped in a particular orthodoxy: that markets are efficient, portfolios should be built to optimize return per unit of risk, and the safest bet for the long haul is to just buy the whole market and wait. This belief system—baked into everything from the CFP® curriculum to the average robo-advisor's algorithm—isn't just widespread. It's sacrosanct. Modern Portfolio Theory (MPT), the Capital Asset Pricing Model (CAPM), and the Efficient Market Hypothesis (EMH) form the Holy Trinity of finance. But like many theological frameworks, these models offer tidy explanations at the expense of messy reality.

Let's rewind the clock to the 1950s, when Harry Markowitz introduced Modern Portfolio Theory in his seminal paper, *Portfolio Selection*. MPT suggested that instead of choosing stocks individually based on expected return, investors should consider how all their holdings interact—their correlations—and aim for an "efficient frontier," where risk-adjusted return is maximized (Markowitz, 1952). It was a brilliant idea. Revolutionary, even. But it came with a catch: it relied on assumptions that are now laughably out of sync with the real world.

Markowitz's model required that investors be perfectly rational, that they all agree on the distribution of returns, and that those returns follow a neat bell curve. In other words, it imagined a world where investors are emotionless robots with perfect data, trading frictionlessly in a market immune to panic. Markowitz himself later acknowledged these assumptions didn't hold in practice, saying, "I should have called it 'An Approximation to Reality'" (Markowitz, interview, 2008). Still, the idea was so elegant—and so quantifiable—that it stuck. Advisors could plug numbers into software, generate pie charts, and look like geniuses.

Building on MPT, the Capital Asset Pricing Model (CAPM) emerged in the 1960s, most notably in the work of William Sharpe (Sharpe, 1964). CAPM sought to explain why some assets offered higher returns than others. It posited that an asset's expected return was a function of its "beta"—its volatility relative to the market. High-beta assets should yield higher returns to compensate for their risk. But again, the model leaned heavily on shaky assumptions: that markets are efficient, investors can borrow and lend at the risk-free rate, and that beta alone captures all relevant risk.

By the 1990s, researchers like Eugene Fama and Kenneth French had already dismantled key parts of CAPM. Their empirical work showed that factors like value (cheap stocks outperform expensive ones) and size (small-cap stocks outperform large-caps) had explanatory power that beta alone could not account for (Fama & French, 1992). These findings didn't kill CAPM, though. In many classrooms and boardrooms, it continued to live on—not because it was right, but because it was useful. CAPM simplified conversations about expected returns, created neat performance benchmarks, and offered a defensible framework when clients asked tough questions.

In 1991, Nobel laureate William Sharpe published a now-famous paper titled *The Arithmetic of Active Management*. In it, he argued that, before costs, the average active investor must earn the same return as the market—and after costs, must underperform. His reasoning was purely mathematical: since the total market is made up of all investors, and passive investors simply hold the market, any active investor who beats the market must be offset by another who lags the market. The average return, by definition, is the market return. Therefore, when active management fees are added, the average active investor must fall short of passive benchmarks over time.

While elegant in theory, Sharpe's conclusion breaks down completely in practice. First, passive investing is not free—it carries costs too, including fees, slippage, rebalancing drag, and tracking error. Second, not all active managers are the same. Sharpe's framework treats them as a homogeneous group, but in the real world, managers differ widely in skill, philosophy, and repeatable process. The existence of high-fee, closet-indexing funds may pull the group average down (i.e. they return the same as passive investments but overcharge for their performance), but that doesn't preclude the presence of high-conviction managers with durable edge. For investors willing to seek them out—or advisors who can build systematic strategies that exploit known market anomalies—the payoff from selectivity can exceed the modest cost differential.

Indeed, a growing body of academic literature challenges Sharpe's fatalism. Cremers and Petajisto (2009) found that funds with high active share—not just hugging the index—tend to outperform. Moreira and Muir (2017) showed that volatility-managed portfolios deliver significantly higher risk-adjusted returns. Hurst, Ooi, and Pedersen (2017) demonstrated the long-term effectiveness of trend-following across global asset classes. These studies and others suggest that when active management is thoughtful, data-driven, and adaptive, it can consistently deliver above-average outcomes. So while Sharpe's arithmetic holds in a closed system of averages, the real world rewards intelligent design.

Yet the simplicity of Sharpe's logic and tautological appeal seeded the most widespread investment narrative of the next generation: *you can't beat the market, so why try?*

That belief found its most dogmatic expression in the Efficient Market Hypothesis. EMH, championed by Eugene Fama in the 1970s, argued that asset prices already reflect all available information (Fama, 1970). In its strongest form, EMH implied that no one could consistently outperform the market, because any edge was instantly priced in. Stock picking? Futile. Market timing? Laughable. Just buy the market and go enjoy your life.

But critics, both academic and practical, have poked holes in EMH for decades. Robert Shiller's work on excess volatility showed that stock prices moved far more than fundamentals could justify (Shiller, 1981). Lo and MacKinlay (1988) found that prices didn't follow random walks, directly contradicting a key tenet of EMH. Behavioral economists like Daniel Kahneman and Richard Thaler demonstrated that investors are often predictably irrational, swayed by biases and emotions, not logic. More pointedly, the existence of anomalies—like momentum (Jegadeesh & Titman, 1993), insider trading profits (Seyhun, 1986), and persistent factor returns (Asness et al., 2014)—undermines the idea that all information is instantly and perfectly priced in.

So why do these flawed models continue to dominate the financial planning industry? The answer lies not in their truth, but in their utility. These theories are *scalable*. They're *compliant*. They're easy to teach, easy to sell, and—most importantly—easy to defend when things go wrong. If a client loses 30% in a downturn, the advisor can point to the benchmark and shrug: "Everyone did." In a profession that's as much about managing liability as managing money, that's a powerful incentive.

But the cracks in the foundation grow more visible with each crisis. During the dot-com bubble, passive investors rode tech stocks all the way up—and then all the way down. Active managers who were paying attention to valuations (and had the flexibility to act) fared far better. In 2008, when diversification across asset classes was supposed to save us, everything collapsed together. Correlations went to one, and passive portfolios offered no safe harbor. Trend-following strategies, however, adapted to market signals and materially reduced drawdowns (Barroso & Santa-Clara, 2015). In March 2020, as COVID-induced panic hit markets, passive funds simply mirrored the plunge. Active, risk-aware strategies reduced exposure early, preserving capital and positioning clients for a stronger recovery (Barclay et al., 2020).

Still, EMH, MPT, and CAPM persist—not because they're accurate, but because they offer plausible deniability. They allow advisors to tell clients, "No one saw it coming," and, "This is the best we can do." These models became the lingua franca of credentialing programs like the CFP® and CFA. And with that institutional endorsement came inertia. Advisors were trained not to question, but to conform.

Then came the Bogleheads.

John C. Bogle, founder of Vanguard and father of the first index fund, transformed EMH from a theory into a movement. In his 1976 launch of the Vanguard 500 Index Fund, he offered investors a product that would simply mirror the market—no research, no forecasting, no fancy footwork. It was derided at first. A Wall Street Journal ad mocked it as "Bogle's Folly." But in time, the fund's ultra-low fees and consistent performance made it a juggernaut. His message resonated: Wall Street is greedy, costs are the enemy, and your best chance at financial success is to avoid doing anything.

The Bogleheads, an online community that grew out of his philosophy, took this to heart. They codified a minimalist approach to investing: buy index funds, ignore the noise, never try to time the market, and above all, keep fees low. While there's wisdom in some of this, the movement became more than practical—it became evangelical. Active managers weren't just wrong; they were villains. Fees weren't just costs; they were sins.

This fervor reshaped the retail investment landscape. Low-cost ETFs exploded in popularity. Advisors were trained to design portfolios by simply mixing index funds based on a client's risk tolerance. Compliance teams cheered—fewer moving parts meant fewer liabilities. Clients nodded along, happy to "own the market" without realizing they also owned its every flaw.

But the idea that *low cost is always better* is built on the same shaky assumptions that powered MPT and EMH. The entire logic hinges on Sharpe's largely disproven 1991 paper, *The Arithmetic of Active Management*. Because active and passive investors collectively *are* the market, and passive investors get the market return, then active investors must underperform the market after fees. Yet we have seen this is false, both logically and academically as has been already stated above. This elegant math only holds under perfect conditions, not real markets: that markets are closed systems (they aren't), that fees are the only difference (they aren't), and that all active managers are essentially the same (they aren't).

Real life is messier. Many active strategies are *not* broadly replicated. They're underutilized or inaccessible to the average investor. Hedge funds, private funds, and family offices deploy capital using information, technology, and execution speed that most retail investors can't access. And critically, some strategies work. Momentum, for instance, has shown statistically significant excess returns across geographies and asset classes (Jegadeesh & Titman, 1993; Barroso & Santa-Clara, 2015). Value investing, while cyclical, persists over long periods. Even tactical allocation strategies can meaningfully reduce drawdowns, boosting long-term compounding even with modest returns.

The problem isn't *fees*—it's *value*. A 2.6% fee sounds high if it buys you nothing. But if it prevents a 40% drawdown, enhances tax efficiency, and gets you back into the market at the right time, it's a bargain. Investors focus too much on cost and not enough on outcome. As Arnott (2012) wrote in *The Glidepath Illusion*, small improvements in risk management—especially near retirement—can have a larger impact on wealth than maximizing average return.

There's also the question of what index funds are actually buying. Take the S&P 500. It's not a thoughtfully constructed portfolio; it's a popularity contest. It holds more of whatever has already grown big, regardless of valuation, sector concentration, or forward risk. In this way, market-cap weighting bakes in momentum in one direction—up—until it breaks. We saw this in the tech bubble, where massive exposure to overpriced tech stocks led to catastrophic losses, and again during the COVID run-up, where the top five stocks accounted for over 25% of the index.

And who benefits from this buy-and-hold orthodoxy? It's not just the investors. Brokers and custodians rake in billions through securities lending. When you own shares in an index fund, those shares are often lent to short sellers, with the revenue flowing to the fund manager—not to you. In 2023 alone, Fidelity reported over $2.1 billion in securities lending income (Fidelity Investments, 2023), most of which was retained by the firm. Schwab's 2025 report showed record profits in their custodial arm, driven in part by passive client assets parked in low-yield sweep accounts (Charles Schwab Corporation, 2025).

Short sellers love passive investors. They're reliable lenders who never call their shares back, even when volatility spikes. Hedge funds can build complex, dynamic strategies on the backs of passive investors, who simply hold through it all. In a very real sense, passive portfolios are the liquidity pool for more sophisticated capital.

Meanwhile, price discovery suffers. Markets work best when participants are constantly evaluating securities and acting on that information. But passive funds don't analyze companies. They don't adjust based on earnings, leadership, or macro conditions. They just buy. As passive ownership rises, fewer shares are actively evaluated, and the price signals become weaker. Studies like Jin & Myers (2006) show that as ownership concentration in index funds increases, R-squared (a measure of how much of a stock's movement is explained by the market) rises, suggesting that stocks are increasingly moving in lockstep—not based on fundamentals, but on flows of money into the market, buying more shares, every two weeks, as 401k contributions from paychecks come in.

In crises, this can turn dangerous. The Flash Crash of 2010, where markets plunged and rebounded within minutes, was exacerbated by the absence of active liquidity providers (Kirilenko et al., 2017). Passive funds don't step in to buy when prices fall; they simply absorb the chaos. As O'Hara (2015) notes, high-frequency traders now dominate liquidity provision, but their algorithms are brittle under stress. When they step back, passive holders are left exposed.

And yet, the narrative persists. EMH, Bogleheadism, and the cult of low cost continue to dominate because they offer something seductive: simplicity. They're easy to teach, easy to replicate, and easy to defend. Advisors can build scalable practices, charge flat fees, and avoid lawsuits. Compliance officers prefer black-and-white rules. And clients like to feel smart for doing nothing.

But simplicity is not the same as safety.

The true cost of this dogma is hidden in the drawdowns—the once-a-decade events that wreck retirements and derail plans. Clients who rode the market down 40% in 2008 or 30% in 2020 weren't comforted by academic theories. They needed portfolios that adapted, advisors who acted, and systems that anticipated.

Active strategies, by contrast, attempt to respond. Not always perfectly, but intentionally. Trend-following models, for instance, are designed to exit or reduce risk when markets break down. During the 2008 crisis, many such strategies were significantly less exposed to the worst of the drawdown. AQR's managed futures program, which incorporates trend signals, posted strong relative returns during that time, while passive strategies absorbed the full force of the collapse (Asness et al., 2014). Similarly, during the COVID crash, funds with systematic de-risking rules reduced exposure weeks before the final leg down, as documented by Barclay, Kaplan, and Lipson (2020).

Yet, these strategies are rarely taught to advisors. The typical CFP or CFA curriculum remains steeped in CAPM, MPT, and the gospel of EMH. Advisors learn to rebalance, not rotate; to diversify, not adapt. Macro awareness, regime analysis, tail risk hedging—these are topics covered in hedge fund whitepapers, not classroom syllabi. The training pipeline itself filters out complexity in favor of what can be neatly tested and certified.

This intellectual ossification means most retail investors are guided by professionals who sincerely believe their only job is to set the initial allocation and stay the course. It's a mindset rooted not in apathy, but in absorption. The industry believes what it teaches, and teaches what is easy to defend.

This is not a neutral failure.

Consider what happens in retirement. A sequence of returns risk means a single market shock early in retirement can devastate future income—even if average returns later are fine. A 30% drop in the first two years of withdrawal can be unrecoverable. Yet most index-based portfolios are designed without any dynamic risk controls. They assume market timing is impossible, so avoiding downturns is futile. But evidence shows this is false.

Lo and MacKinlay (1988) famously demonstrated that stock prices do not follow a random walk. Momentum strategies have shown statistical significance in producing excess returns across decades and geographic regions (Jegadeesh & Titman, 1993). Even simple moving-average models—buy above the 200-day, sell below—have consistently reduced drawdowns without destroying returns (Barroso & Santa-Clara, 2015). These aren't speculative black-boxes—they're published, peer-reviewed, and reproducible.

The tragedy is that much of this knowledge has migrated *upstream*. Hedge funds, family offices, endowments—they're not constrained by the narrative of EMH. They use models, adjust exposure, and apply forward-looking risk signals. They build portfolios to behave in specific ways across regimes. Retail clients, meanwhile, are told to hold 60/40, rebalance annually, and hope the averages work out.

This divide isn't just philosophical. It's structural.

Advisors have been boxed in by product design, compliance regimes, and fee compression. AUM fees are simple, so portfolios must be simple. ETFs are easy to implement, so they became the default building block. Advisors aren't rewarded for building resilient systems—they're rewarded for staying in their lane. The result: advisors sell beta, while institutions pursue alpha.

Consider this: if indexing is so clearly superior, why do sophisticated investors still hire active managers? Why do pension funds allocate billions to tactical mandates, multi-asset overlays, and alternative strategies? Why do hedge funds, despite their fees, continue to attract institutional capital? It's not because they all expect to beat the market every year. It's because they believe that *intelligent structure* can outperform *unstructured exposure* over time—especially when adjusted for risk.

This belief is supported by behavior research too. DALBAR's *Quantitative Analysis of Investor Behavior* (2021) shows that the average equity investor underperforms their own investments—by over 2% annually—due to poor timing and emotional decisions. A system that limits drawdowns not only improves the return path; it helps clients *stay invested.* In that way, a risk-aware strategy may deliver better outcomes *even if the headline return is the same.*

And yet, clients rarely hear this argument. They're told the enemy is fees, that markets can't be predicted, and that deviation is dangerous. It's tidy. It's humble. But it's wrong.

Take the S&P 500 again. In 1999, it was overloaded with tech stocks, many of which had no profits. In 2007, it was bloated with financials, right before the mortgage crisis. In 2021, it concentrated heavily in Big Tech just before a massive sector rotation. Passive portfolios never ask if their holdings make sense—they just buy what's biggest. This isn't diversification—it's drift.

And that drift has real costs. When the market corrects, these portfolios offer no brakes. The investor rides every bump and cliff. No system, no signal, just hope. Meanwhile, institutions run multi-factor models that integrate macro data, volatility signals, and sentiment analysis. They don't avoid losses completely—but they manage them. And over time, this makes a difference.

But retail investors were sold a different story. They were told complexity was dangerous, that trying to adapt was futile, and that low cost was the same as high value. They weren't wrong to believe it. The story was compelling. But it wasn't complete.

There is a better question than "Is this portfolio cheap?" It's "Does this portfolio work *when I need it most*?"

Because a portfolio is more than a bucket of assets. It's a system. One that should be designed with intention, tested across regimes, and monitored for adaptability. It should anticipate—not predict—how different environments affect different exposures. And it should be built to protect, not just to grow.

There is another way.

Smart investors—those who think like owners, not renters—ask different questions:

- **What's the logic behind my portfolio?** Is there a model, or just a mix?

- **How does it handle stress?** Does it adapt when conditions change?
- **Is anyone accountable for results?** Or is my advisor just tracking a benchmark?
- **What are institutions doing that I'm not?** And why?

These are uncomfortable questions in a world that prefers low-cost sameness. But they are the right ones.

Because real investing is not just about "being in the market." It's about positioning—what you own, when, and why. It's about understanding that *drawdowns hurt more than fees*. That *behavioral mistakes destroy more value than expense ratios ever did*. And that *systems beat slogans*.

The myth of simplicity serves many—but not the client.

A smarter approach doesn't reject indexing—it transcends it. It uses ETFs as tools, not strategies. It applies evidence-based methods to manage risk, exploit inefficiencies, and align portfolios with real-world goals. It understands that complexity didn't disappear—it just moved upstairs.

And most of all, it dares to believe that financial advice can be about *excellence*, not just *execution*.

Because in a complex world, simplicity isn't a virtue. It's a vulnerability.

Chapter 8

Designing Dynamic Portfolios

Most investors think portfolio management is as simple as picking an allocation, rebalancing once a year, and staying the course. That model fits neatly in textbooks and CFP exam prep materials, but it tends to fall apart the moment it meets real-world volatility. Markets shift. Liquidity dries up. Correlations break or converge. A pie chart built for one regime quickly gets crushed in another. And still—most investors do nothing. Most advisors do the same. The premise of this chapter is simple: to survive in real markets, you need a portfolio that can adapt.

So why can't you just buy an active management strategy?

Not all investment strategies are available to everyone—and that's by design. Most of the world's best-performing, actively managed portfolios are gated by sky-high minimums, legal structures, or both. They're not listed on your brokerage app. They don't advertise during the Super Bowl. And unless you walk in with eight figures and a polished financial statement, they don't want your money. Why?

There are two reasons. First is regulatory: the U.S. Securities and Exchange Commission defines *accredited investors* as those with a certain income or net worth, under the assumption that wealthier individuals can better understand, tolerate, and afford the risks that come with complex or non-transparent investments. Many hedge funds, private equity shops, and active strategies take full advantage of this exemption, choosing to stay private to avoid the compliance burden of being publicly accessible. That's the legal half.

The other half is human. When an investor with $50,000 loses 20%, they panic. It's not just numbers—it's rent, retirement, college savings, and identity. They email, they call, they demand answers. That same 20% drawdown on a $100 million portfolio? It still stings, but it doesn't threaten their lifestyle. The investor may be annoyed, but they're not scared. That psychological difference translates into a massive difference in behavior—and workload. As a result, many investment managers who run volatile or uncorrelated strategies, which may underperform the market in some years, intentionally set their minimum investment levels high—not just to attract more dollars, but to attract a specific kind of investor: experienced, patient, and emotionally stable.

Academia backs this up. Research by Barber, Odean, and others has shown that less affluent investors are more prone to panic selling and performance chasing . Further, studies on *investor sophistication* (Campbell, 2006; Gennaioli et al., 2015) find that wealthier investors tend to better understand risk, are more likely to hold diversified portfolios, and less likely to make emotion-driven changes. From the fund manager's perspective, this reduces friction, call volume, and fire drills. In short, high minimums are not just an economic filter—they're a behavioral one.

None of this means lower-net-worth investors are incapable of handling risk. It just means the system is built to reward scale and emotional discipline—traits more common among the wealthy, either by training or by insulation. The good news? That doesn't mean you're locked out. It means you need to find—or build—systems that emulate the same discipline, logic, and structure that institutional capital enjoys. That's what this chapter is about.

A dynamic portfolio doesn't try to predict the future—it responds to what's already observable. It reads the signals and responds. Think of it as weather-aware flying. You don't guess the weather. You read the radar. You shift altitude or route based on turbulence, wind, and storms ahead. In investing, that means adapting to current market regimes, volatility conditions, macroeconomic signals, trend direction, and valuation environments. This isn't a speculative exercise. It's data-driven and grounded in decades of academic literature.

Let's break it down. First, market regime classification. Any truly dynamic portfolio begins with understanding the environment it operates in. Markets don't exist in a vacuum—they oscillate between risk-on expansions, late-cycle caution, crisis panics, and recovery periods. Each of these regimes behaves differently. For example, during an expansion, volatility tends to be low and momentum strong. Conversely, during a crisis, volatility spikes and credit spreads widen. Identifying the regime requires quantifiable inputs. These might include the slope of the 200-day moving average, the level and term structure of the VIX, changes in credit spreads (such as the high-yield option-adjusted spread), shifts in the ISM Purchasing Managers Index (PMI), and earnings revision breadth.

To illustrate, suppose we define a few formulas to help classify regimes:

$$\text{PMI}_{\text{slope}} = \text{PMI}_{\text{current}} - \text{PMI}_{\text{3mo avg}}$$

$$\text{Momentum Score} = \left(\frac{\text{Price}_{\text{today}}}{\text{Price}_{\text{200DMA}}}\right) - 1$$

$$\text{Credit Spread Change} = \text{HY OAS}_{\text{current}} - \text{HY OAS}_{\text{1mo ago}}$$

Once a regime is identified, the next step is asset selection tailored to that specific environment. During risk-on periods, equities—especially small-cap and high-beta stocks—tend to outperform. In late-cycle markets, when valuations are high and earnings begin to decline, value stocks, defensive sectors, and gold often provide better protection. When markets descend into panic, capital preservation becomes paramount, making Treasuries, cash, and even volatility hedges more attractive. As recovery begins, assets with strong momentum—like credit-sensitive instruments or cyclicals—tend to lead.

This brings us to volatility targeting. Instead of holding fixed percentages in various asset classes, dynamic portfolios adjust position sizes based on current risk. If one asset suddenly becomes more volatile, its allocation is reduced to keep total portfolio risk within acceptable bounds. The formula is straightforward:

$$\text{Position Weight} = \frac{\text{Target Volatility}}{\text{Realized Volatility}}$$

For example, if your target volatility is 10% annually and an asset currently exhibits a 20-day realized volatility of 15%, your weight for that position becomes…

$$\text{Position Weight} = \frac{10\%}{15\%} = 0.6667$$

Trend-following overlays add another dimension of defense. These filters aim to avoid the most catastrophic drawdowns by exiting or reducing exposure when trends reverse. Antonacci's Dual Momentum strategy combines relative momentum (comparing performance of assets like SPY vs. EFA vs. AGG) and absolute momentum (whether 12-month return is positive). If neither test is met, it shifts into cash or defensive positions. Another filter might simply say: if the price is below the 200-day moving average and the VIX is above 30, reduce equity exposure by 50%.

With signals in place, the question becomes: how do you allocate capital?

One approach is risk parity, where assets are weighted by volatility contribution rather than capital. If stocks are twice as volatile as bonds, a 50/50 risk contribution might result in a 25% allocation to stocks and 75% to bonds.

$$\text{Weight}_{\text{stock}} = 0.5 \cdot \left(\frac{10}{20}\right) = 0.25$$

$$\text{Weight}_{\text{bond}} = 0.5 \cdot \left(\frac{20}{10}\right) = 1.0$$

Alternatively, a max Sharpe optimization solves for the following objective function:

$$\max \quad \frac{w^T \mu - r_f}{\sqrt{w^T \Sigma w}}$$

subject to

$$\sum w_i = 1, \quad w_i \geq 0$$

Where w is the weight vector, μ is expected returns, r_f is the risk-free rate, and Σ is the covariance matrix.

Rebalancing and execution round out the system. Dynamic doesn't mean daily fiddling. You can rebalance monthly or when signals cross thresholds. Use tolerance bands to reduce unnecessary turnover, like rebalancing only when a position drifts 5% from its target. And always factor in taxes and transaction costs. Execution matters.

Why does all this work? Because markets are conditional. The S&P 500 does not return 10% every year. Some years it returns -37%, others +28%. By dynamically adjusting exposure to match the regime, volatility, and valuation, you reduce drawdowns, maintain upside participation, and improve compounding.

Designing a dynamic portfolio isn't easy. It requires math, code, and discipline. It doesn't always win. Some years you'll trail a static benchmark. But over time, the ability to adapt to market conditions rather than simply ride them out creates resilience—and results.

If you want a portfolio that adapts to crises, inflation, and policy shocks—one that tilts toward survival and longevity over blind faith—you need more than a pie chart. You need a system. You need to design.

My own dividend optimization portfolio was built based on a 25-page academic paper that I wrote and then implemented in about 1,000 lines of multi-threaded Python code. If you have the training and skill, you can do this, too.

But what if you read this chapter and thought, "I'd rather just buy this strategy than make it myself?" Stay tuned and keep reading. I'll give you the answer in this next chapter.

CHAPTER 9

A SMARTER FUTURE FOR FINANCIAL ADVICE

Most investors ask the wrong question. They want to know, "What's your return this year?" As if investing were a sport and the scoreboard updated quarterly. But that's not the question that matters—not if your goal is to reach the finish line intact. That's like evaluating a surgeon based on how fast they operate. Speed might be impressive, but not if it compromises the outcome.

A better question—the real question—is: "What system do you use to protect and grow capital across all conditions?" Because great investing isn't about this year's leaderboard. It's about building something that lasts through storm and cycle, through decades of change. It's not a sprint; it's a long, unpredictable journey. One that demands more than optimism or convention. It demands a plan.

Let's dispel the myth of constant outperformance. No system, no matter how sophisticated or statistically backed, outperforms every year. Momentum strategies stumble in sideways markets. Value underperforms during growth-fueled rallies. Even well-constructed macro trend portfolios can lag when the signals are muted. The best strategies in the world have off years—sometimes terrible years. But their value isn't in those occasional stumbles. It's in what happens during the years that matter most: the years when markets break.

In a -30% market, a portfolio that declines only -15% preserves far more than capital—it preserves opportunity. From a smaller loss, the recovery runway is shorter and steeper. A -30% drop requires a +42.9% gain to get back to breakeven. A -15% drop? Just +17.6%. Even if the more conservative portfolio underperforms in the rebound, it can still come out ahead, simply because it didn't fall as far in the first place. That's not an opinion. That's math. And that's why the right system isn't judged by its average annual return alone—it's judged by how it behaves when everything breaks.

That's what investors often miss: the rebound advantage. It's the quiet, compounding result of avoiding catastrophe. It's not as flashy as the headline return in a bull year. But over a full cycle, it's the edge that matters most.

So the next time you meet an advisor, skip the question about performance last year. Ask instead: "What's your process for managing risk in a regime change?" Ask them what macroeconomic indicators they monitor. Ask how they adjust risk exposure when volatility spikes. Ask whether they rotate between sectors, factors, or assets when conditions shift. Ask what signals trigger rebalancing—and how often they test their system for robustness. If the answer is some version of "We don't try to predict" or "We just stay the course," then you're not talking to a strategist. You're talking to a placeholder.

A real investment system is more than a static pie chart. It integrates risk models—volatility targeting, drawdown thresholds, stress testing. It adapts allocation to changing conditions, incorporating trend signals, valuation spreads, and macro regimes. It includes protocols for what to do when the world turns upside down. That's not market timing. That's engineering.

You're not paying your advisor for this quarter's return. You're paying them for the architecture—the framework that determines your outcome over the next ten years. A good system is built with intention. It anticipates failure points. It diversifies not just by asset class but by behavior under stress. And it remains coherent when the noise gets loud.

Of course, this brings us to fees. That 2.6% fee often triggers a reflexive wince. It feels high, especially compared to the index advisors who charge a fraction of that. But the question shouldn't be "What does it cost?" The real question is "What am I getting in return?"

If your advisor hands you a basic ETF portfolio and rebalances it quarterly, 2.6% is far too much. You're paying luxury pricing for a mass-market product. But if your advisor is running multiple risk models across timeframes, dynamically reallocating based on macro and trend data, applying volatility overlays to manage drawdowns, and integrating your tax strategy, withdrawal plan, and estate goals into every portfolio decision—then 2.6% might be a bargain.

Value is not the absence of cost. It's what you get for the cost you pay. And in this case, it's not just better returns—it's better resilience.

Behavior, too, is part of the equation. One of the most underappreciated values of a true advisory system is behavioral architecture. Not in the sense of handholding, but in the sense of structure. The greatest enemy of compounding isn't poor returns—it's human error. Panic selling in a crisis. Buying the hottest fund after a rally. Freezing when decisive action is needed. These are not hypothetical risks. They are well-documented patterns, and they destroy more wealth than any fee ever charged.

An advisor who arms you with a system—who helps you understand what to expect, what to do, and why it matters—gives you more than advice. They give you discipline. They turn impulse into strategy. And they save you from mistakes that could cost hundreds of thousands in missed opportunity.

Think of it like this: a -30% behavioral mistake—say, selling at the bottom of a bear market—requires a +43% return just to recover. That mistake, avoided once, just paid for years of advisory fees.

Still, not all advisors are created equal. And the industry, unfortunately, has done much to commoditize itself. But excellence still exists. Some advisors are deeply trained in macroeconomics, capital markets, and behavioral finance. They build adaptive engines that evolve with new data. They tie your investment plan to your life goals—not just your risk tolerance questionnaire. Others? They simply track the market.

Excellence is rare. It's expensive to build. But it's priceless to experience. And it's worth seeking out, even if it costs more than you expected. Because when the time comes to make the hard decision—to hedge, to rotate, to de-risk, to stay in—it won't be a spreadsheet that saves you. It'll be the system. And the human behind it.

At Fireweed Capital, we don't believe in outsourcing your future to a rebalancing algorithm. We design systems that think. That adapt. That stress test the world not as we wish it to be, but as it is. We use tactical overlays for volatility, momentum, and macro shifts. We build recession-aware models and inflation-sensitive tilts. We run simulations not just for "normal" years, but for years like 2008, 2020, and 2022. And we integrate those models into client-specific plans that tie directly into what matters to you.

This isn't magic. It's just real work. Real engineering. Real planning. We don't claim to know the future. We claim to be prepared for it. And if that's the kind of investing you want—not a guess, not a gamble, but a grounded system—then I'm ready to talk.

Because in the end, great investing isn't about one good year. It's about surviving all the bad ones and emerging stronger. It's not about being right—it's about being prepared. And that's what a system gives you.

Not just growth. But resilience. And peace.

If you're ready to stop guessing with your portfolio and start working with someone who actually has a system—reach out and let's talk.

FURTHER READING AND WORKS CITED

Antonacci, G. (2014). *Dual momentum investing: An innovative strategy for higher returns with lower risk.* McGraw-Hill Education.

Arnott, R. (2012). The glidepath illusion. *Research Affiliates.* https://www.researchaffiliates.com/en_us/publications/articles/162_the_glidepath_illusion.html

Arnott, R., Hsu, J., & Moore, P. (2005). Fundamental indexation. *Financial Analysts Journal, 61*(2), 83–99. https://doi.org/10.2469/faj.v61.n2.2718

Asness, C., Frazzini, A., Gormsen, N. J., & Pedersen, L. H. (2014). Understanding style premia. *AQR Capital Management.* https://www.aqr.com/Insights/Research/Working-Paper/Understanding-Style-Premia

Barclay, M. J., Kaplan, S. N., & Lipson, M. (2020). The performance of U.S. exchange traded funds during the COVID-19 crisis. *Journal of Banking & Finance, 122,* 105983. https://doi.org/10.1016/j.jbankfin.2020.105983

Barroso, P., & Santa-Clara, P. (2015). Momentum has its moments. *Journal of Financial Economics, 116*(1), 111–120. https://doi.org/10.1016/j.jfineco.2014.11.010

Bengen, W. P. (1994). Determining withdrawal rates using historical data. *Journal of Financial Planning, 7*(4), 171–180.

Charles Schwab Corporation. (2025). *Q2 2025 financial results.* Schwab Investor Center. https://www.schwab.com/investor-relations

DALBAR Inc. (2021). *Quantitative analysis of investor behavior.* https://www.dalbar.com

DALBAR Inc. (2022). *Quantitative analysis of investor behavior.* https://www.dalbar.com

Daniel, K., & Moskowitz, T. J. (2016). Momentum crashes. *Journal of Financial Economics, 122*(2), 221–247. https://doi.org/10.1016/j.jfineco.2016.01.002

Fama, E. F. (1970). Efficient capital markets: A review of theory and empirical work. *Journal of Finance, 25*(2), 383–417. https://doi.org/10.2307/2325486

Fidelity Investments. (2023). *H1 2023 securities lending income disclosure.* Fidelity Institutional. https://institutional.fidelity.com

Goldman Sachs. (2024). *Annual prime brokerage report.* Goldman Sachs Publications.

Hurst, B., Ooi, Y. H., & Pedersen, L. H. (2017). A century of evidence on trend-following investing. *Journal of Portfolio Management, 44*(1), 15–29. https://doi.org/10.3905/jpm.2017.44.1.015

Jegadeesh, N., & Titman, S. (1993). Returns to buying winners and selling losers: Implications for stock market efficiency. *Journal of Finance, 48*(1), 65–91. https://doi.org/10.1111/j.1540-6261.1993.tb04702.x

Jin, L., & Myers, S. C. (2006). R squared around the world: New theory and new tests. *Journal of Financial Economics, 79*(2), 257–292. https://doi.org/10.1016/j.jfineco.2004.11.003

Kirilenko, A. A., Kyle, A. S., Samadi, M., & Tuzun, T. (2017). The flash crash: High-frequency trading in an electronic market. *Journal of Finance, 72*(3), 967–998. https://doi.org/10.1111/jofi.12538

Kitces, M., & Pfau, W. D. (2014). Reducing retirement risk with a rising equity glide-path. *Journal of Financial Planning, 27*(1), 38–45.

Kritzman, M., Li, Y., Page, S., & Rigobon, R. (2012). Principal components as a measure of systemic risk. *Journal of Portfolio Management, 38*(4), 112–126. https://doi.org/10.3905/jpm.2012.38.4.112

Lo, A. W. (2004). *Adaptive markets: Financial evolution at the speed of thought.* Princeton University Press.

Lo, A. W., & MacKinlay, A. C. (1988). Stock market prices do not follow random walks: Evidence from a simple specification test. *Review of Financial Studies, 1*(1), 41–66. https://doi.org/10.1093/rfs/1.1.41

Moreira, A., & Muir, T. (2017). Volatility-managed portfolios. *Journal of Finance, 72*(4), 1611–1644. https://doi.org/10.1111/jofi.12505

Moskowitz, T. J., Ooi, Y. H., & Pedersen, L. H. (2012). Time series momentum. *Journal of Financial Economics, 104*(2), 228–250. https://doi.org/10.1016/j.jfineco.2011.11.003

O'Hara, M. (2015). High-frequency trading and the new market makers. *Journal of Financial Markets, 16*, 712–740. https://doi.org/10.1016/j.finmar.2015.09.003

Seyhun, H. N. (1986). Insiders' profits, costs of trading, and market efficiency. *Journal of Financial Economics, 16*(2), 189–212. https://doi.org/10.1016/0304-405X(86)90060-7

Seyhun, H. N. (1992). The effectiveness of insider trading regulations. *Journal of Law and Economics, 35*(1), 149–182. https://doi.org/10.1086/467245

Sharpe, W. F. (1991). The arithmetic of active management. *Financial Analysts Journal, 47*(1), 7–9. https://doi.org/10.2469/faj.v47.n1.7

Shiller, R. J. (1981). Do stock prices move too much to be justified by subsequent changes in dividends? *American Economic Review, 71*(3), 421–436.

Shiller, R. J. (2000). *Irrational exuberance*. Princeton University Press.

Souza, B. D., & Venkatesan, S. (2021). Trading behavior and price discovery. *Journal of Financial Markets, 54*, 100630. https://doi.org/10.1016/j.finmar.2020.100630

About the Author

If you want financial advice from someone who's lived it, not just studied it, I'm the right person to call. As founder of Fireweed Capital, I help clients build and protect wealth with clear, practical guidance. I hold the AAMS® and CRPC® designations, a Bachelor's degree in Finance, a Master's degree in Cybersecurity, and a Doctorate in Computer Science.

My journey into financial advising began fresh out of college, but I quickly realized that I felt like an imposter, advising clients without having proven strategies myself. This led me to spend the next decade learning and earning through real-world experiences. During this time, I was involved in three company sales and an IPO, which taught me invaluable lessons about what my clients need to build their financial lives.

Before founding Fireweed, I spent a decade investing my own money learning what actually works (and what doesn't!) across stocks, bonds, real estate, private credit, private equity, venture capital, and angel investments. That real-world experience shaped how I advise today.

I work with professionals and families who want more than cookie-cutter plans. If you're looking for a financial guide who's walked the path first, let's talk.

- Dr. Adam Link

Disclaimer

The author is an Investment Advisor Representative and fiduciary under applicable laws and regulations. However, no fiduciary or advisory relationship is created by reading this book. The information provided is for general educational and informational purposes only and should not be interpreted as personalized investment, financial, tax, or legal advice.

This book does not establish a client relationship with the author or Fireweed Capital. All investment strategies involve risk, including the potential loss of principal. Past performance does not guarantee future results. Readers should consult their own financial advisor, tax professional, or attorney before making any decisions based on this content.

Examples, case studies, and client stories are illustrative and may be fictionalized or modified to protect confidentiality. Any references to performance or investment outcomes are not promises or predictions of future results.

Fireweed Capital is a licensed insurance agency. Adam Link provides insurance services to clients through Fireweed Capital, which is separate from Dr. Link's role as an investment advisor representative of Portfolio Medics. Investment advisory services are offered through Portfolio Medics. Fireweed Capital and Portfolio Medics are not affiliated.

Made in the USA
Las Vegas, NV
19 September 2026

ae8a1cfa-6256-4001-afff-3d93ef5d3afdR01